" Behold the fruits, the flowers, the leaves and the branches..."

(Verlaine)

Twenty-seven fragrant herbs, some exotic and some familiar
(hyssop, balm, coriander, saffron, thyme, artemisia, angelica...),
distilled together drop by drop to achieve the vigour,
the aroma, and the unique flavour of Bénédictine;
the ideal liqueur for creating the spontaneity and warm, natural
atmosphere of charm on every occasion
from a quiet evening with friends to a formal dinner.

The Guest of Honour at all receptions,
Benedictine, is pleased
to ofter you this specially compiled
"Guide to Perfect Entertaining".

CONTENTS

For the hostess...

For the host...

Just for two.

Benedictine

For the Hostess

Successful entertaining is an art, an art full of secrets and... some recipes. Of course, you should know some general rules and proven formulas. But a bit of imagination and fantasy can give your entertaining that indispensable personal touch.

The menu, the decor, the atmosphere of the evening will reflect your personality and ensure its success.

Do remember that it's often the little details which establish your reputation as the perfect hostess and make your reception an enjoyable event for your guests... and for yourself.

Large formal dinner setting

This is the occasion for the hostess to decorate her table with great care.

The Traditional Table Setting

Decide on the number of guests, and consider the size of your table as well as your dining room. That way, you will be certain that all guests will have sufficient space and that they can be served with ease.

— A large tablecloth should be chosen instead of place mats.

— A white tablecloth is no longer a must; a coloured one in harmony with your plates can be used.

— One or two plates per person.

Between courses, the used plates should be replaced immediately with clean ones so that there is never an empty table.

— Preheat the plates before serving hot dishes.

— Place the forks on the left of the plate, the knives on the right.

— Beside the forks, place individual breadplates with a butter-knife inside the main knife.

— Fish knives and forks are put outside the main fork and knife.

— Dessert cutlery is normally placed in front of the plate.

— A glass for each wine should be provided for each guest, with the water glass at the left of the wine glass.

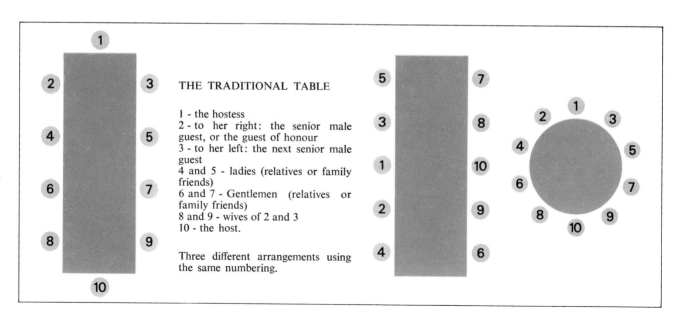

THE TRADITIONAL TABLE

1 - the hostess
2 - to her right: the senior male guest, or the guest of honour
3 - to her left: the next senior male guest
4 and 5 - ladies (relatives or family friends)
6 and 7 - Gentlemen (relatives or family friends)
8 and 9 - wives of 2 and 3
10 - the host.

Three different arrangements using the same numbering.

— Don't forget salt, pepper, butter, individual ashtrays and lighters, bread-baskets.

Fingerbowls with warm water and lemon should be made available after a course of shellfish or asparagus.

— Napkins matching the tablecloth, simply folded lengthwise, are placed on the plate.

No Heavily Scented Flowers

Harmony is very important. Do not mix gold and silver, rustic and elegant plates, etc.

— A reserved decor is best: perhaps a lovely silver centre-piece, flowers, leaves or fruit arranged in low bowls.

— Don't choose too heavily scented flowers.

— Place small circular bouquets on a round table, or at each end of a long table.

— On a white or pastel tablecloth, you may use very colourful flowers. With white plates on a coloured table-cloth, choose flowers of a similar tone.

— Place high candelabras at the ends of a long table. White candles in a silver candelabra are very elegant, but candle colour may be matched to either the tablecloth or the plates. Remember to choose dripless candles.

— Indicate seating arrangement with small name cards at each place.

Separate the Couples

The host and hostess sit opposite each other, with the guests to their left and right; always separate the couples.

At a long table the host and hostess may sit either at the heads of the table or across from each other at the middle. This avoids having all less important guests at one end of the table.

Each dish is served from the left of each guest, beginning with the lady seated to the right of the host, followed by the one on his left and concluding with the hostess. The gentlemen are then served, starting with the one on the hostess's right and ending with the host.

If convenient, provide a separate table for the children, with the older ones taking care of the younger.

FORMAL TABLE SETTING "à la française"

A variety of informal settings

A delightful idea to be reserved for your more intimate friends, the young ones —in spirit at least.

Lovers Tête-à-Tête

— Plan for two to six people per table, never more.

— Separate the couples and the jealous ones. ... plan!

Make only one exception to this rule : when the dinner is given for newly-weds or for a recently engaged couple, they may be seated at the same table.

— Try to have an equal number of young men and ladies at each table. If there are more ladies than gentlemen, why not make sure the party's Don Juan finds his place in their midst?

— In any case, try to have a good « mixer » at each table.

The Essential Ingredient: Your Imagination

This time, the atmosphere is most important. Give free reign to your imagination. Here are some suggestions:

"Pub Style". Imitate the decor of your favourite pub. Simple tablecloths and napkins, sturdy glasses for the beer, or perhaps "à la française" with pitchers of wine, a bread basket, an arrangement of condiments and a handwritten menu. You could even dress up as innkeepers. To complete the image, the hostess serves the dishes as the host fills the glasses.

"The Opposites". Have a completely different setting for each table; you'll find the contrast delighful and conversation provoking.

The Romantic Table. It should be a round table, with a long, fancy table-cloth, a soft light that highlights the precious china. Place a rose on each lady's plate and use a romantic cluster of flowers as a centre-piece.

The Rustic Table. Have a boldly checked tablecloth, earthenware and mugs. A rustic lantern and either gaily coloured wild flowers or dried leaves in a stone jug for decoration.

The Scandinavian Table. Place coloured place mats on a teakwood table, use ultra-modern plates, cutlery and glasses. A wood or metal shaded lamp and stylized flowers complete the Scandinavian look.

The Lovers' Table. Choose a pastel coloured tablecloth, classic plates, candles for soft light and red roses in a heart shaped bowl.

One Course Dinner

With a large number of guests and several tables, you will be wise to simplify dinner as much as possible. This is a perfect occasion for a huge sauerkraut dish, a stew, or a spaghetti and meatball dish.

Afterwards, you may offer a large choice of cheeses and different desserts, fruits and/or ice cream. Add to this the proper background music to create a general good mood and you will be assured of a perfect evening.

The t.v. party

How often have you heard, or even said it yourself, "Television spoils everything; we don't go out anymore, or see our friends..." But after all, couldn't you use a favourite T.V. programme, a show or game, or election results for example, as a get together with your friends? Go ahead —**Organise a T.V. Dinner!**

A word of advice: Unless you want a debate filled evening, don't invite people of radically differing opinions. Even the most perfect gentleman might get carried away when caught up in his favourite subjetct.

Cushions For The Young Ones

Avoid making your living room look like a cinema. Instead of having several straight rows of chairs, group them around low tables, where your guests can find cigarettes and ashtrays, and place plates and glasses.

The younger guests can sit either on cushions in front of your T.V. or right on the carpet. Avoid bright lights; instead, place a soft light above or behind your television and several others at different locations in the room.

No Knives and Forks

Have a large selection of drinks on hand: whisky, cocktails (see recipes pages 40-43), champagne or dry white wine, beaujolais, beer, fruit juices, coca-cola, mineral waters and sodas.

You can serve anything that's easily eaten without knives and forks: olives, salted crackers, dried fruit, almonds, salted nuts, radishes, sticks of celery, all kinds of canapes, with salmon, ham or chicken. Also any cold meats, with cheese, cubed cheese with celery salt. Depending on the season, fruits such as cherries, plums, apricots, raisins, clementines, are excellent. Don't

forget to include some desserts, little tarts and fancy biscuits.

Tray Meal and Self Service

The meal on a tray is popular for informal friendly evenings. Moulded trays in plastic or light metal similar to the ones used by some airlines would be perfect. You could prepare them all in advance.

As your guests arrive, offer them drinks and a comfortable place to sit, with cigarettes and ashtrays at hand. Also arrange snacks (olives, nuts and potato crips) on small tables near their seats.

Before the programme starts, hand everybody his tray and refill the glasses. You might also have a buffet close by where each guest could help himself to canapes and pastries. The rest is easy; all you have to do is replenish glasses and plates from time to time during the programme's lighter or less exciting moments.

The surprise party

Any number of friends —close or not so close— with bottles, food and records under their arms, dropping in on you as you were about to take a bath —that was the "surprise party" of the wild twenties. But nowadays a surprise party can be almost anything, from a snobbish cocktail party to a hippie reunion.

Psychedelic Decor

Once the carpet is rolled up, big lamps and furniture moved aside to clear the dancing area, and all fragile knickknacks out of reach, you have all the freedom you need to decorate imaginatively. Try a cluster of plants in one corner, flowers in stable, sturdy vases and lots of colours: balloons in red, green and yellow, psychadelic designs, posters...
To avoid any stains on your furniture, make sure to have multicoloured papermats with gay patterns —animals, proverbs, cocktail recipes. Your guests will be happy to place their glasses on them. Keep cigarettes, ashtrays and matches handy throughout the room. Group chairs and cushions around low tables for resting and exhausted dancers.
Little or no heating; have plenty of ventilation; use smoke-absorbing candles.
Don't forget a cloak room; anyone wanting to leave early should be able to find his coat without too much trouble and without breaking up the party.

Lots of Rock

Have plenty of pop records on hand, some for dancing and others that are pleasant just for listening.
Think about the non-dancers too. Maybe some amusing games will do the trick. As soon as the first guests arrive, put on a lively record to create the mood of the party.

And Very Important: Warn your neighbours ahead of time, or invite them too.

Plenty to Drink and Lots of Party Snacks

Even though nobody comes for the buffet alone, its variety of food and drinks will ensure the success of your party.

The drinks: Whisky and soda, gin and tonic, champagne, cocktails - choose some recipes you are quite sure of (see pages 40-43). Fruit juices, soft drinks and mineral waters. A Sangria or an iced punch are always appreciated. A small barrel of Beaujolais or a keg of beer, where everybody can help himself go well with a country style buffet.

NOTE THAT:

1 bottle of whisky serves about 15 glasses
1 bottle of champagne serves about 5 glasses
1 bottle of aperitif serves about 10 glasses
1 quart of fruit juice serves 6 glasses

Have plenty of ice cubes ready and more in the refrigerator for refills. Lots of different cocktail snacks are always welcome: salted nuts, black and green olives, cheese cubes with celery salt, potato crisps, dries figs, raisins, etc.

Prepare all kinds of Canapes: With salmon, caviar, salami, foie gras, ham, cucumber, cottage cheese with

herbs, celery sticks with roquefort cheese, little cocktail sausages with mustard.

For those with a sweet tooth: Little fruit tarts, French pastries, small Danish pastries, candied fruits and biscuits. Have about six canapes and six sweets per person, and about 4 pounds of nuts, olives, etc., for eight people.

If you are able to serve ice cream or fresh fruit salad, you'll please a large number of your guests.

This is more or less the classic way of preparing a buffet; there is an almost infinite number of other solutions however.

— If you are able to make fondue, you can offer your friends either a fondue savoyarde (cheese) or a fondue bourguignonne (meat).

— Another suggestion: have a rustic buffet, where you serve mainly cold cuts, sausages and cheeses.

— And of course, you can combine any of our hints with your own special ideas.

The Spotlight is on...

...your buffet!. This is usually a long table, placed about a yard from the wall, to permit the "barman" to work at ease. The table is best covered with a large tablecloth that hangs down to the floor in front to hide additional bottles, glasses and iceboxes, which are easily accessible from behind the table. You could just as easily use several small tables. Here is the usual arrangement:

— Bottles and glasses, champagne glasses and whisky glasses (the latter being also used for cocktails and fruit juices).

— Canapes and biscuits on trays or long serving dishes.

— Bowls of nuts, olives and crackers.

— Deep plates for cocktail sausages.

— Fruit baskets.

— Dessert plates, tea spoons, forks and paper napkins.

— Ashtrays and bowls for cocktail sticks and wastepaper.

— Cigarette and toothpick holders.

Use colourful and imaginative things for your glass markers: little clothes-pegs, coloured tabs or labels with letters or numbers.

It's a lovely decoration to have pineapples or grapefruits covered with coloured plastic sticks holding olives, cheese cubes and sausages.

An Attractive Hostess

Arrange everything well in advance so as to have a moment to yourself before your guests arrive. Take care of your make-up and hair-do. Dress without haste. It's quite fashionable now to wear a comfortable gown or even a slightly exotic outfit.

Welcome each of your guests as they arrive with your warmest smile. Introduce the ones who don't know each other. Don't forget those who have a tendency to stay alone in their corner. Put everyone at ease and have a good time.

The garden party

If the sun co-operates, this is defintely the party that is everybody's favourite, host's and guest's alike.

You don't need a big park for it; if you have a garden with broad paths, or a nice lawn, or even just a large terrace with plants all around, don't hesitate: plan a garden party.

Simplicity and Abundance

Fancy decorations are not necessary. Just place chairs and tables conveniently in the shade of trees or under parasols. Decorate your buffet with branches and flowers and have gaily coloured lounge chairs placed here and there.

For background music, choose either a record player with plenty of records or else a tape recorder.

A wheelbarrow might be a novel idea for a rolling bar. Buckets filled with ice will keep your bottles cooled:

whisky, cocktails, champagne. A small barrel of Beaujolais or a keg of beer in a cool corner of your garden will certainty be a welcome sight. Be sure to have plenty of mineral water and fruit juices on hand.

For the buffet: a country style table-cloth, no delicate plates or silverware, but instead, coloured plates, rustic tumblers, serving platters in teak or olive wood, wicker baskets and piles of paper napkins.

Don't prepare any canapes. Set up patés in dishes, salami, sausages, ham, cold chicken and cold cuts, mustard, gurkins and spices. Add all the raw vegetables you like: carrots, celery stalks, radishes, small onions, tomatoes, etc. Mixed salads with rice, noodles or potatoes. Present a selection of cheeses on a platter and in a bowl, cottage cheese with garlic and herbs.

Serve also a large variety of fresh fruit and pastries.

Don't forget a large assortment of bread, white and brown, in slices, and plenty of butter.

Self Service

Each guest can help himself to whatever he chooses. The gentlemen can share the serving of drinks while the ladies fill the plates, and a general good humour will spread easily through your party.

If you really want to surprise your friends, have a suckling pig or a lamb roasting on a spit in one corner of your garden. Here again, encourage your guests' participation. As one is tending to the fire, another can watch

the cooking. Have someone skilled in carving take over that responsability, and everyone can help in handing around the plates.

For the evening, have the lighting ready:

A mushroom shaped lamp in the centre of your lawn will give a very pleasant low light. Place a bright spotlight above the buffet, candle-light lanterns on the tables, strings of multicoloured lights and Chinese lanterns strung from tree to tree. Don't forget to have some scented powders or papers that you can burn to ward off flies and mosquitoes.

Hopefully, the weather will be as enjoyable as the time, your guests will have. But just in case, have a room prepared for an emergency transfer of buffet, bar and guests so that the party can continue indoors if needs be.

The barbecue

A name that goes all the way back to the corsairs of the Caribbean Seas, who had the rather unpleasant habit of roasting their prisoners on a large framework called the "barbacoa". Luckily customs have changed, and nowadays "barbecue" simply means roasting the carcass of beef or pork out-of-doors. Slowly it has even become the name given to any meal grilled on a charcoal fire.

A barbecue is a favourite for country houses, be it out in the garden, on a terrace, or even in a large fire place. Many different and savoury recipes have been developed for barbecue cooking and the host can create them anew in front of his appreciative guests.

The Spit or The Grill

All kinds of different barbecue models are sold: little cast-iron ones for the terrace, the fold-up barbecue, easily put up and easy to transport; trans-formable barbecues, where the top is a grill and the sides will roast the meat on a spit; the permanently built one with a wind shade; a large gridiron, and of course, you can always build your own.

Some Basic Principles

Have a well ventilated charcoal bed with a capacity of at least 4 lbs. of charcoal. There should be no wind on the embers and the barbecue should be so arranged that the smoke blows away from the guests.

What to Have on Hand

— Some lighting fluid to start your fire, either half a glass to sprinkle over the coal, or else some cotton wool soaked in the fluid.

— Coarse salt thrown over the fire can be used to regulate the fire.

— A dozen skewers.

— A spit with a battery-run roasting jack, which can be adapted to a special appliance for turning the skewers as well.

— A cas-iron griddle.

— Two grills with long handles, one for fish, the other for meat. Double grills are easier for turning the meat over.

— Utensils with long handles, such as: a fork and a pair of tongs for turning the meat, a brush for basting, and a shovel for the embers.

— A large cutting board and a well sharpened knife.

Embers and Aromatic Herbs

To prepare the barbecue light the fire at least 20 minutes in advance and

begin the roasting once the charcoal has turned white. Flames shouldn't touch the meat; a small branch dipped in water will help you to keep the flames down, or you can throw some ashes over the fire to moderate it.

A vertical grate is very useful for larger and greasier pieces of meat. The spit should turn in front of the heat allowing the meat juices to drip into a pan below.

If you throw herbs like thyme, rosemary or fennel into the fire, the meats, vegetables or fish will take on a delicious aroma.

Use plenty of pepper, saffron, spices and flavourings and have a choice of sauces on the table: with garlic or onion, different mustards, pickled gerkins and onions.

SOME BARBECUE RECIPES

- Grilled sardines - small grilled herrings *(4 per person)*
Clean and turn them in flour, then place them on a hot grill for 3 minutes on each side while throwing some branches of thyme and rosemary into the fire.
Serve with lemon slices and fresh butter.

Grilled trout with fennel
Clean, flour and baste the fish. Grill it over a fire with fennel in it.

Roast lamb *(2 chops per person)*
Let the roast turn slowly on a spit for 20 to 30 minutes, while throwing aromatic herbs into the fire.

Rib of beef *(for 4 persons)*
Soak aromatic herbs in oil then spread the oil over a rib of beef and place it on a very hot grill. Turn it over after about 10 minutes. Pepper generously and serve with small grilled tomatoes.

Barbecued poultry
Chicken and duck are quite delicious when roasted on a spit, as well as guinea-fowl if you bard it first.
Cooking time: about 45 minutes. The poultry should have a golden crust and secrete a clear juice when you test it with a fork.

Garnishings:

Grilled vegetables: tomatoes, red and green peppers, mushrooms, aubergine, and most of all: **baked potatoes.** Take big potatoes, wrap them in aluminium foil, bake them in the embers. For serving, cut them open crosswise and put a lump of butter or sour cream inside.

Skewers *(plan on 2 skewers per person)*
— **Scampi skewers:** having shelled the scampi, soak them in a mixture of oil, pepper and herbs. Put them onto the skewers and grill them over a very hot fire for approximately 5 minutes.

— **Sausage skewers:** to prepare the skewers, alternate pieces of sausage with small tomatoes and mushrooms. We suggest trying a spicy sausage like pepperoni. Baste well and grill for about 5 minutes.

— **Lamb skewers:** Alternate cubes of lamb, kidneys, smoked bacon, green peppers, onions and tomatoes on the skewers and grill over very hot fire for about 5 minutes.

Just for two

It could be for his birthday, for yours, or for your wedding anniversary, or simply for your own pleasure: a special evening at home. Offer yourselves a honeymoon dinner just fort the two of you.

Leave the Telephone off the Hook

Be sure both of your are free of any professionnal, social or family obligations. Don't hesitate to doublelock your door, take the telephone off the hook, for this is one evening dedicated solely to each other.

Give the house a festive look: flowers in all vases, soft lights and if possible a wood fire in the fire place.

In a cosy corner, a small table lit by candlelight, set with your most precious china, crystal and silverware. Nothing is too beautiful for this evening. Next to his plate, a small gift, wrapped and tied with ribbons. A few suggestions: A record that both of you would enjoy, another pipe for his collection, the book he has wanted to read for so long, your photo in a leather frame for his desk, or a funny gadget...

Don't forget the background music. Next to the record player have ready all the records you both enjoy hearing.

The menu: a Bit of Extravagance

Don't spend your time in the kitchen today. Order your dinner from a catering service and set it up near your table on a sideboard or a tea-trolley within easy reach. Choose the dish that you both love best; don't hesitate to have little extravagances like caviar, served with iced vodka; or foie gras, oysters, a tarragon chicken, an exotic salad, a choice of fine cheeses, his favourite dessert, fresh fruit, anyhow — a dinner without problems.

The champagne should be in an ice bucket on a tray. You should have everything prepared for the later hours of the evening: small French pastries, mocha cups, liqueur bottle and glasses.

Temptation and Surprise

All you have to do now is to prepare yourself for this evening. Be tempting and different. Surprise him with a new hair style, or even a wig, that will transform you into an entirely different woman for one evening. Choose a hostess gown in soft colours and flowing material, jewelry that enhances your sparkling eyes and don't forget to wear the perfume he loves most.

Desserts

To make the syrup, boil the water and the sugar for a few moments, then add the B AND B.

You can garnish the Baba with whipped cream.

BANANA FLAMBÉ WITH B AND B

Take six firm bananas and roll them in granulated sugar. In a frying pan, melt 100 grams of butter and fry the bananas until golden all over. Add 4 spoonfuls of B AND B. Arrange the bananas on a warmed dish, sprinkle with the juice and ignite for serving.

BENEDICTINE CREAM BISCUITS

For the dough: 400 grams of flour, 250 grams of butter, 2 eggs, 200 grams of sugar, 2 grams of yeast, a pinch of salt.

For the cream: 100 grams of butter, 100 grams of fondant, 100 grams of

BABA WITH B AND B

250 grams of flour, 15 grams of yeast, 1/8 litre of milk, 2 eggs, 20 grams of granulated sugar, 75 grams of butter, a pinch of salt.

For the syrup: 300 grams of sugar, 1/3 litre of water, 2 glasses of B AND B.

Prepare the dough in a deep bowl with lukewarm milk, sugar, yeast, and only half the flour. Cover the dough and let it stand in a warm place until it doubles in volume. Add the remaining ingredients and knead them together until an elastic and smooth dough is achieved. Allow to stand for another 10 to 15 minutes, then fill half a cake pan. Allow the batter to rise to the rim of the pan before baking in a moderate oven for 20 minutes. Let it cool for a while, turn out and pour the warm syrup over the Baba.

Banana flambé with B and B

chocolate cream, 1/8 litre of Benedictine, glazed sugar.

To prepare the batter: Add the ingredients to the sifted flour, knead well and let the mixture set for two hours. Roll the batter into a sheet 1/8 inch thick. Cut out discs 1 1/2 inches in diameter, placing them onto a buttered baking tin and bake in moderate oven. For the cream: Thoroughly Mix the butter, fondant, chocolate cream and Benedictine.

Spread a thick layer of cream onto half of the cooled round biscuits. Top these with the others and coat them by rolling in icing sugar.

CHESTNUT CREAM WITH BENEDICTINE

Prepare a custard with 1/2 litre of milk, 4 egg yolks, 125 grams of sugar and 50 grams of flour.

200 grams of chestnuts cooked in vanilla flavoured milk and reduced to puree consistency.

Biscuits soaked in Benedictine, whipped cream, bits of Marrons glacés.

Cook the mixture of custard and chestnut purée. Pour an inch-thick layer into a deep dish, cover with a layer of biscuits and continue alternating the cream and the biscuits to fill the dish. Allow it to cool. Decorate with whipped cream and pieces of Marrons glacés.

CREPE BENEDICTINE

(for 25 crepes) 250 grams of sifted flour, a pinch of salt, 75 grams of granulated sugar, 3 whole eggs and 2 egg yolks, 5 centilitres of Benedictine, a twist of lemon.

Mix the ingredients and let the mixture set for a few minutes. Add 40 centilitres of lukewarm milk and allow to cool before adding 65 grams of melted butter (golden brown). Allow to stand for an hour before making the crepes.

CREPES SUZETTE WITH B AND B

Prepare thin crepes with a batter flavoured with 2 tablespoons of B AND B.

In a chafing dish, melt 6 tablespoons of sugar and blend in 6 teaspoons of butter. Fold the crepes in quarters and turn them in the hot sauce. Pour orange syrup and warmed B AND B over the crepes and ignite before serving.

To prepare the orange syrup: Boil the juice of 4 oranges and 1 lemon with

Mocha cake with Benedictine

200 grams of sugar, a twist of orange and a dash of grenadine.

DESSERT OMELETTE
WITH B AND B

12 eggs, 2 tablespoons of sugar, a glass of B AND B.

Beat the eggs well, slowly adding the sugar. Cook as you would normally cook an omelette. Then sprinkle

BANANA OMELETTE

12 eggs, 3 bananas, sugar, B AND B.

Slice bananas and fry them in butter. Prepare an omelette as in the above recipe and add the banana slices before folding the omelette in half. Slide onto a preheated chafing dish, sprinkle

with sugar, pour over the B AND B and ignite just before serving.

PECHES FLAMBÉES

2 pounds of peaches, apricot gelatine, B AND B.

Poach the halved peaches in hot syrup. Cover the peaches with apricot gelatine flavoured with B AND B. Warm some B AND B and pour it over the preparation and ignite for serving.

This recipe can also be made with pears. You may use fresh fruit as well as tinned.

FRUIT SALAD
WITH BENEDICTINE

Apples, grapefruit, pears, peaches, lemon juice, 5 centilitres of Benedictine.

Dice the fruit, add lemon juice and Benedictine. Put into the refrigerator for at least an hour before serving.

with sugar and B AND B, and ignite just before serving.

ICE CREAM WITH B AND B

1 litre of milk, 1 vanilla bean, 300 grams of sugar, 8 egg yolks, 1 decilitre of B AND B, 150 grams of preserved fruit steeped for 2 or 3 days in B AND B.

Melon surprise

Boil the milk with the vanilla. In a bowl mix the sugar, egg yolks and the B AND B; whip it well into a light batter. Pour in the boiling milk while stirring. Heat it all again for one minute and allow to cool. Add the fruit and place in the freezer compartment.

ICED MERINGUE
WITH BENEDICTINE

4 egg whites, 250 grams of sugar, butter-cream, fondant, Benedictine.

Beat the egg whites stiff, adding the juice of one lemon. Gradually add the sugar. Do not allow the whites to collapse. Fill a meringue mould with this mixture. Place in the oven at its lowest setting.

Remove from the mould when cooked and glaze the upper part with fondant which has been warmed and softened with Benedictine. Top off with chocolate cream.

MELON SURPRISE

A ripe melon, strawberries, bananas, sugar, Benedictine.

Slice off the top of a melon and empty out the water and seeds. Scoop out the inside and cut it into cubes. Add an equal amount of strawberries and sliced bananas. Sprinkle with sugar and flavour with Benedictine. Toss this fruit salad and fill the melon shell with it.

Replace the top and let cool in the refrigerator.

MOCHA CAKE
WITH BENEDICTINE

One Genoese cake, 300 grams of moka

Rice pudding with fruit

cream, Benedictine, chopped burnt almonds (one cupful).

Slice the Genoese cake into two or three layers according to its thickness. Flavour with Benedictine, then insert between two layers of cake one two-centimetre layer of mocha butter cream, keeping a little of the cream for decoration. Cover the sides with chopped burnt almonds and decorate the top of the cake with the remaining butter cream.

ORANGES WITH BENEDICTINE

4 oranges, 1 package of wafers, 1 1/2 cups of whipped cream, 4 tablespoons of Benedictine, blanched and chopped almonds.

Cut the top of the oranges. Scoop out inside, keeping the juice. Mix the whipped cream, Benedictine, sugar, almonds and four tablespoons of orange juice. Fill the oranges with this mixture, replace the top and let cool in refrigerator. Garnish with wafers for serving.

RICE PUDDING WITH FRUIT

150 grams of rice, 1/2 litre of milk, 1 stick of vanilla, 100 grams of granulated sugar, 2 egg yolks, 20 grams of butter, fruits in season (apples, peaches, apricots, cherries).

Cook rice in milk with vanilla. Add the sugar, the egg yolks, and stir well. Cook for a moment at low heat and continue to stir until milk is absorbed. Let cool and arrange in a circle on a serving dish. Decorate with fruits and coat with gooseberry jelly softened with Benedictine.

ROAYL STRAWBERRIES

150 grams of rice, 1 litre of milk, 150 grams of granulated sugar, strawberries and strawberry jelly, Benedictine.

Cook the washed rice in boiling milk for about 20 minutes. Add sugar and bring to boil again. Pour into deep tube-pan and let cool in the refrigerator. Turn out and decorate the ring interior with strawberries. Cover with strawberry jelly flavoured with Benedictine.

BENEDICTINE SORBET

200 grams of sugar, 400 grams of water, juice of one lemon, 1 decilitre of Benedictine, 175 grams of sugared whipped cream.

Make a syrup with the water, sugar and lemon juice. Allow to cool, then place into refrigerator. When the sorbet has set, add the whipped cream and the Benedictine, mixing all the ingredients well. Serve in tall champagne glasses.

BENEDICTINE SOUFFLE

2 decilitres of milk, 60 grams of sugar, 40 grams of starch, 20 grams of butter, 4 egg yolks, 5 egg whites, 1 pinch of salt, Benedictine.

Boil the milk with the salt. Add the starch diluted with a little milk and the sugar. Cook for two minutes. Remove from the heat and blend into the mixture the egg yolks and the butter, then the egg whites (beaten very stiff) and the Benedictine. Put in a buttered soufflé mould and sprinkle with sugar. Cook in medium oven for 20 minutes.

Fruit soufflé

Any fruit you care to choose may be added to the above soufflé, after being chopped and steeped in Benedictine.

Iced meringue with Benedictine

For the Host

The winecellar and the bar are under the care of the host. But they involve a big responsability, calling for good judgement, taste and quite a bit of knowledge. A well stocked winecellar, choosing the right wine for dinner, the set-up of your bar, selecting liqueurs and spirits, mixing cocktails, serving the drinks... none of these complex and delicate things should be unfamilar to you.

Although the hostess is in the limelight at a reception, your talents will be appreciated and the connoisseurs will always remember that remarkable Pomerol 1949 you served with the duck, or the warmth of the Bénédictine they enjoyed during friendly evenings together.

A well stocked winecellar

Isn't the well stocked winecellar with its reputed bottles the dream of any host? That dream can be fulfilled, but take some precautions.

Well Aged Wines

Wine is a living and delicate thing. Even once it's bottled, it continues its evolution. Good conditions will enhance the ageing, whereas a long stay in a bad winecellar can kill your wine.

The ideal winecellar should be:
— cool, with an even temperature from 50º to 54ºF;
— well ventilated;
— not too dry and not too humid. Slight humidity is preferable to complete dryness;
— without any strong smell;
— with a strong foundation, preferably an earth floor, or a cement floor that should be moistened frequently. If your cellar is not entirely up to these standards, be sure to at least stack your bottles in a cool, airy corner, away from central heating boilers; such storage could be disastrous to your wine.

A Good Wine

Choose good quality table wines that you can drink young and fresh. Famous wines of noble origins will be an honour at your table.

Unless you are an expert, avoid buying your wine in barrels. You are wiser buying wine of a good year, bottled by the grower, after it has fermented the right amount of time in oak barrels. Bottling origins are indicated on the label as follows: for the Bordeaux - "mise en bouteille du viticulteur" = bottled by the grower, or "mise en bouteille au château" = bottled at the chateau. For the Burgundies - "mise en bouteille du domaine" = bottled at the estate. The stamped and dated cork will confirm this.

As for champagne, the initials on the label have a precise meaning:
R.M. - Récoltant Manipulateur = distributed by the wine grower.
N.M. - Négociant Manipulateur = distributed by the shipper (Négociant).
M.A. - Marque Auxiliaire = auxiliary brand or "Buyer's own Brand".
C.M. - Coopérative de Manipulation = distributed by co-operative.

Beware of Overageing

Your bottles will age well in your cellar if you store them in racks or lying on shelves. Separate the different wines, knowing that a red is better at a higher temperature (59º) than a white. All wrappings —paper or straw— should be removed, as they might absorb humidity and transfer it to the cork, which can possibily give the wine a musty taste. Be aware of the fact that great Bordeaux and Burgundy wines reach perfection only after 5 or 6 years. But don't overage your wines. Those forgotten about bottles from a hidden store will give forth only a wine of poor taste and flavour.

To guide your choice for your winecellar:

Diagram of the qualities of French wines by régions and years with respect to their evolution.

YEARS	Red Bordeaux	White Bordeaux	Red Burgundy	White Burgundy	Cotes du Rhone	Alsace	Pouilly s Loire Sancerre	Anjou Touraine
1924	★	•••	•••	••	••			••
1926	•••	•••	••••	•••	•••			
1928	★	•••	•••	•••	••			••••
1929	••••	••••	★	••	••			••
1934	••	•••	••••	•••	•••			•••
1937	••	★	•••	••••	••			••••
1943	••	•••	•••	•••	••			•••
1945	••••	•••	•••	•••	••	(OUT OF STOCK)	(OUT OF STOCK)	
1947	••••	••••	••••	•••	•••			★
1948	•••	•••	•••	••	••			
1949	••••	•••	••••	•••	•••			
1950	••	•••	•	•••	••			
1952	••	•••	•••	••	••••			••
1953	••••	•••	•••	•••	••			•••
1955	•••	•••	•••	•••	••			••
1957	••	•••	•••	•••	••			•••
1959	••••	•••	••••	•••	••			••
1960	••	••		•	••			••
1961	★	•••	••••	••••	••••	••••	•••	•••
1962	•••	•••	•••	•••	•••	•••	•••	•••
1964	••••	•••	•••	•••	•••	•••	•••	••
1966	••••	•••	••••	•••	•••	•••	••	••
1967	•••	••	•••	•••	•••	••		••
1968	Not recorded - Some good quality wines							
1969	Very promising in certain régions - Young wines with bouquet have been much appreciated.							

Medium Year •	Good Year ••	Very Good Year •••	Great Year ••••	Exceptional Year ★

Classification applies to the average - exceptions confirm the rule.

Harmonizing Food and Wine

There is, as you well know, a subtle agreement between wines and food. Nevertheless, there are no absolute rules; nothing can stop you from experimenting according to your own personal taste. Reputed gastronomes have been seen to serve a young Beaujolais with oysters, a Côtes du Rhône with Bouillabaisse, or a Sauternes with Fondue.

Others prefer not to change wines during dinner and will serve only one kind.

As a general rule, three wines are served at a formal dinner:
— a dry white wine with the appetizer, also appreciated as an aperitif.
— two red wines.

You may add a sweet wine with the dessert; a Sauternes of a good year, for example. Champagne is always right and equally appreciated as an aperitif.

A Few Guidelines in Choosing a Wine:

With seafood, eggs, and fresh-water fish:
— Burgundy (white): *Chablis (delicious with oysters), Meursault, Montrachet, Pouilly-Fuissé, Mâcon.*
— Bordeaux: *white Graves, Château Haut-Brion, Château Virelade.*
— Dry white wines from the Loire valley: *Muscadet, Coteaux du Layon, les Pouillys.*
— All the wines from Alsace: *(perfect with foie gras) Traminer, Tokay, Gewurztztraminer.*

— White or rosé wines from the Jura: *(ideal with trout and fresh-water fish).*
— Wines from Provence: *Cassis (with Bouillabaisse and fish) Rosé de Porquerolles.*

With red meat:
— Red Bordeaux *like Saint-Emilion.*
— Red Burgundy from the Côte de Beaune *(Volnay, Corton, Pommard)* etc., or from the Côte de Nuits *(Nuit-Saint-Georges, Vosne Romanée, Clos de Vougeot, Chambolle-Musigny, Gevrey-Chambertin...).*
— Beaujolais: *Morgon, Brouilly, Moulin-à-vent.*
— Wines from the Chalonnais: *Mercurey, Givry.*
— Wines from the Rhône valley: *Hermitage...*
— Red wines from the Jura: *Arbois.*

With white meat:
— Bordeaux: *red Graves and Médoc.*
— Red wines from the Jura: *wines from Arbois.*

With poultry and Game:
— Bordeaux: Saint-Émilion.
— Burgundy from the Côte de Beaune: *Volnay, Corton, Pommard.*
— Wines from the Chalonnais: *Mercurey.*
— Wines from the Rhône valley: *Hermitage, Châteauneuf-du-Pape.*

With Cheeses:
— Bordeaux: *white Sauternes*
— Burgundy *from the Côte de Beaune and the Côte de Nuits.*
— Beaujolais: *Morgon, Brouilly, Moulin-à-vent.*
— Wines from the Chalonnais: *Mercury...*

— Wines from the Rhône valley: *Hermitage, Châteauneuf-du-Pape*.
— Wines from Périgord: *red Bergerac*.

With desserts:

— White Bordeaux: *Sauternes with cake, ice cream and fruits.*
— White wines from the Loire valley: *Coteaux du Layon with dry biscuits.*
— Wines from Périgord: *Monbazillac and white Bergerac.*
— Wines from the Jura: *vin jaune and vin paille served chilled.*

Also quite appreciated as aperitif.

Wines: Chilled or at Room Temperature

When you choose your wines for your reception, take them from your wine-cellar, handling them gently, especially the venerable bottles. Warm or chill them accordingly.
— It only takes about 15 minutes to bring your opened red wine to room temperature if your room is heated at about 68º.
— Don't chill your wines for too long in the refrigerator and avoid the freezer; an ice-bucket is preferable.

Ideal Temperatures:

— Full red wines: no more than 65º
— light red wines: 61º
— Beaujolais: 54º
— white wines: 50º as an average
— Champagne: 41 to 43º
— Sauternes: close to 32º

Remember that tasting the wine before serving it to your guests is part of the host's duties.

A drink at the bar

It is important to group all your aperitifs, liqueurs, and spirits as well as an assortment of glasses and the necessary accessories, to have them all close at hand. There are plenty of places to set up your bar: a piece of furniture with a flap, to prepare the drinks on; a tea rolley converted into a rolling bar for your living room. If you have plenty of space, have a real built-in bar with a refrigerator, shelves for the bottles and glasses and a working surface. Situate it either in a corner of your living or dining room, or even better a small adjacent room opening to your living room.

Individual Decoration

To create the right atmosphere, have some high bar-stools and your individual decoration. Anything goes: advertisments of wines and beers, posters of the gay twenties, play-bills, etc. Why not have your children and friends design some bottle labels for you? Have some gadgets, like bottle-imps, mobiles and balloons to amuse your friends. Or you can keep strictly to one kind of style, for instance:

Boat style: mahogany, thick ropes, fishing nets, anchors and hurricane lamps.

The tropical bar: Bamboo, raffia, exotic flowers and plants, lamps made of moonfish.

The french bistro: a zinc counter and French picture posters.

The saloon: with its typical swinging doors.

The pub: leather, engravings, a dart board.

A Good Assortment of Drinks

Some basic bottles may be sufficient, but for a well stocked bar, where you are able to mix a large number of cocktails and satisfy your guests' preferences, you'll need a good assortment of bottles.

— **Aperitifs:** Porto, Banyuls, sweet and dry aperitif wines, vermouth.

— **Spirits:** Cognac*, Armagnac, Cherry Brandy (or other flavours), Whisky, Vodka, Gin, white and gold label Rum.

— **Liqueurs:** Benedictine, a herb based liqueur, and B AND B (mixture of Benedictine and Cognac), Pippermint Get, or fruit based liqueurs: orange, currant, cherry, etc.

— **Syrups:** sugarcane syrup, grenadine syrup.

— **Mixes:** soda, tonic water, coca-cola. You'll need eggs, milk, celery salt, nutmeg, twists of lemon, a peppermill, granulated sugar.

— **Fruit juices:** orange, lemon, grapefruit, pineapple, tomato.

— **Beer:** stout and ale, light and strong, for everybody's taste.

Some Basic Accessories

— A shaker for cocktails based on syrups, juices, eggs or milk;

— a tall glass with a long spoon to stir the less concentrated cocktails;

— an ice-crusher, a grater for fruit rinds, a large bucket for cooling the bottles, an ice-bucket with tongs, glassmarkers, straws, eggbeater, corkscrews and tin-openers.

All Purpose Glasses

For your bar you have the same choice of glasses as you have for the table. Either the formal, more or less precious set, or else the modern all purpose glasses, plain or decorated.

---

* **INITIALS AND INDICATIONS ON COGNAC BOTTLES, EXPRESSING THE QUALITY RESULTING FROM AGEING:**

— ★★★ : good Cognac of standard quality

— **V.S.O.P. "Very Superior Old Pale":** high quality cognac, having matured a long time in oak casks and has obtained an amber colour.

— **"Reserve" or "Vieille Reserve":** superior cognac with an even longer ageing period in oak casks.

"*A sublimated aroma
of angelica and hyssop
blended with iodous
seaplants and languished
with sugar.*"
(*J.K. Huysmans*)

Here are the distinctive bottles with their amber liqueur, prepared from the five centuries old secret recipe using 27 wild, exotic plants and fruits blended with selected alcohols.

Benedictine is the truly great liqueur, an after-dinner drink of subtle aromas and magnificent fragrances.

The way to enjoy Benedictine is to sip it slowly and quietly. Play your favourite record, smoke a good cigar and sit, with your glass of Benedictine, in a comfortable armchair. Just close your eyes, relax and think of the splendour of Normandy's wonderful countryside as you savour the world's most enjoyable liqueur.

To double your pleasure, share it with a friend. Or hold a big Benedictine and B AND B party.

At the end of a meal serve them straight into previously chilled glasses. During the day your friends will enjoy them as long drinks in highball glasses with two ice-cubes.

As an aperitif, Benedictine and B AND B will add colour and warmth to your cocktails. And don't forget that souffles and desserts also provide connoisseurs with a thousand ways of appreciating the flavour and aroma of Benedictine and B AND B.

Cocktails

ABBEY
- 1/4 Benedictine
- 1/4 red Cinzano
- 1/4 dry Cinzano
- 1/4 Gin

ACACIA
- 2/3 Gin
- 1/3 Benedictine
- 1 dash of Kirsch

ALSACE DREAM
- 1/2 Prunelle
- 1/4 Cherry Rocher
- 1/4 Comandon Cognac
- 2 dashes of Benedictine

BADALONA
- 1/3 Benedictine
- 1/3 Picon
- 1/3 Pippermint Get

BALLERINA
- 1/2 Martell Cognac
- 1/2 Benedictine

BOIS ROSE
- 1/3 B and B
- 1/3 Noilly Prat
- 1/3 Black Currant Liqueur
- 1 slice of lemon

CARUSO
- 1/3 Noilly Prat
- 1/3 Gin
- 1/3 Pippermint Get

COCKTAIL CHAMPION
- 3/10 Noilly Prat
- 3/10 Whisky
- 2/10 Benedictine
- 2/10 white Curaçao

D.O.M.
- 1/4 lemon juice
- 1/4 Benedictine
- 1/2 Comandon Cognac

DRY MONASTIC
- 2/6 Benedictine
- 3/6 red Cinzano
- 1/6 Gin

ETCHE SPI
- 1/2 grapefruit juice
- 1/2 Benedictine

FANCY BENEDICTINE
- 1 glass of Benedictine
- 2 dashes of Angostura
- 2 sponfuls of water
  chilled glass

GLAD EYE
- 1/3 Pippermint Get
- 2/3 Aniseed

GOLDEN FLEECE
- 1/2 Benedictine
- 1/2 eau de vie de Dantzig

GREEN GRASSHOPPER
- 1/3 Pippermint Get
- 1/3 Cocoa Liqueur
- 1/3 cocentrated milk

GREEN LIGHT
- 1/2 Pippermint Get
- 1/2 dry Gin

HURRICANE
- 1/4 Whisky
- 1/4 Gin
- 1/4 Pippermint Get
- 1/4 lemon juice

Etche Spi

IRRESISTIBLE
- 1/2 red Cinzano
- 1/4 Benedictine
- 1/4 lemon juice

Knickenbein

RAINBOW

1/5 Strawberry Liqueur
1/5 Cherry Rocher
1/5 Pippermint Get
1/5 Benedictine
1/5 Kummel

RED LION

1/3 Black Currant Liqueur
2/3 Whisky
   2 dashes of Benedictine
   2 dashes of Pernod

ROTOTO

2 dashes of Cognac
2 dashes of Curaçao
2 dashes of Benedictine
2 dashes of Maraschino
fill with white wine
garnish with fruit

Spring

KNICKENBEIN

1/2 glass of Vanilla **Liqueur**
add one egg yolk **without**
breaking it, pour **along**
the edge without stirring:
1/2 Kummel
1/2 Benedictine
   1 dash of Angostura

MADONNA

1/4 Benedictine
1/4 Médoc Liqueur
1/4 Kummel
1/4 Ginger Brandy

MARCEL'S CUP

1/3 rosé wine
1/3 Benedictine
1/3 Comandon Cognac
   1 slice of orange
   1 peel of cucumber
   1 peppermint leaf
   soda

Marcel's Cup

SAINT-TROP

1 bottle of Schweppes
1 large glass of **Benedictine**
1 slice of orange
serve chilled

SANTIAGO SHAKE UP

1/4 Benedictine
1/4 Rum
1/2 Curaçao

SCAFFA RUM

1/2 Rum
1/2 Benedictine
   2 dashes of Angostura

SPRING

3/5 Gin
1/5 Benedictine
1/5 Dubonnet
   1 olive

STARBOARD FIRE
1/3 Pippermint Get
2/3 Vodka

Turlututu

STRAITS SLING
4/6 Gin
1/6 Cherry Brandy
2 dashes lemon juice
1 dash Curaçao
1 dash of Angostura
soda water

TURLUTUTU
1/3 Benedictine
1/3 dry Cinzano
1/3 Vodka
1 dash of Angostura
1 cherry

TROPICANA
2/3 grapefruit juice
1/3 dry white wine
1 spoonful of Benedictine
1 spoonful of lemon juice

VEL D'HIV
3/5 Comandon Cognac
1/5 Benedictine
1/5 lemon juice
1 dash of Angostura

VELVET FLAMES
1/5 Comandon Cognac
1/5 Cherry Rocher
1/5 Benedictine
1/5 Kummel
1/5 Ginger Brandy

VIKING
2/3 B and B
1/3 Noilly Prat
1 zest of lemon

WHISKY SCAFFA
1/2 Benedictine
1/2 Whisky
1 dash of Angostura

BENEDICTINE ON CRUSHED ICE
Fill half of highball glass with crushed ice, fill up slowly with Benedictine. A very refreshing, deliciously tasting drink, to be sipped with a straw.

BENEDICTINE MILK SHAKE
1/4 litre of milk, 50 grams of sugar, 1 cup of mixed, diced fruit, 2 egg yolks, 100 g of iced cream, Benedictine.

Blend ingredients in mixer, serve on ice, 2 spoonfuls of jam can replace the fruit.

44 - Benedictine - "Guide to perfect entertaining"

BENEDICTINE FECAMP NORMANDY

A general view of the town may be obtained by climbing the Côte de la Vierge towards the chapel of Notre-Dame du Salut. From this hill the whole of the seaside town can be seen lying at the foot of the white cliffs: the long shingle beach, the docks and the cluster of grey roofs from which rise three tall pinnacles: the sturdy lantern tower of the abbey church, the square belfry of St-Etienne and the graceful slender spire of the Benedictine distillery and museum.

Visitors make their first stop in the Place des Ducs Richard to appreciate the beauty of the Abbey Church of the Trinity, the architectural jewel of the town: it possesses a nave in a remarkably pure style, a transept with a fine lantern surmounted by a beautifully proportioned Norman Gothic tower, and a choir with a triple bay beyond which there extends an apsidal chapel in flamboyant Gothic style. These magnificent features together with the curious additions of a Louis XV facade still bear witness to the importance of the famous abbey which was destroyed during the French Revolution.

The port really only comes to life in January when the celebration of the great "Newfoundland Pardon" takes place or in December when the boats return with their heavy load of cod for the Fécamp fish-drying industry.

The real centre of attraction as is shown by all the notices appearing along the approach roads and streets of the town is "The Benedictine Museum and Distillery". At the end of the narrow street named "Alexandre Le Grand", quite near a flower-bedecked square in which stands the statue of Dom Bernardo Vincelli, the creator of the Benedictine elixir, visitors are immediately impressed by the magnificent and ornate Gothic and Renaissance design of the buildings which house the Benedictine Distillery and museum. A fine monumental staircase opening on to a spacious courtyard provides a welcoming feature of the design.

The world-wide fame of Benedictine

Ever since 1863, Benedictine's success has been growing and its fame has rapidly spread to other countries.

In 1938, in order to meet a demand for dryer alcoholic drinks, B AND B (Benedictine and Brandy) was perfected. Combining the delicate flavour of the liqueur with the aroma of a fine cognac, B AND B has acquired world-wide fame.

Today both products are known and appreciated in all countries.

In 1969, more than 80 % of the total production was exported. Together Benedictine and B AND B account for the exports of 30 % of French liqueurs and the figure for the U.S.A. is of over 50 %.

Thus it is that the distinctive bottles containing Benedictine and B AND B carry the reputation for high quality French products from New York to Rio de Janeiro, from Singapore to Dakar, from Hong Kong to London, from San Francisco to Rome.

The glorious history
of the Benedictine abbey

In the district known as Caux on the coast of Normandy, at the foot of the cliffs covered with aromatic herbs, lies Fécamp Abbey, which had been founded in 658 and became, in the Middle Ages, one of the holy places of Normandy. It had a succession of famous abbots and priors, but the world-wide fame which it still enjoys today is due to a monk who was also a herbalist.

About 1510 the monk, Dom Bernardo Vincelli, was studying, herbs, plants and spices, the only pharmacopoeia then known. With the primitive means at his disposal, soaking, heating, mixing, adding predetermined quantities of angelica and hyssop, balm and all the aromatic herbs gathered near the abbey, he succeeded in compounding a remarkable elixir.

"Upon my faith, I never tasted better!" declared King Francis 1st after a visit to Fécamp Abbey during which the monks, anxious to please and honour him, had offered him a glass of the unique elixir prepared by Dom Bernardo.

The formula of this marvellous liqueur in which plant juices were blended to form a liquid the colour of amber and with an unsurpassable flavour was written down on parchment and preciously guarded by the monks who handed down from generation to generation the secret of its manufacture.

Then came the revolution which shook the whole of France, swept away the religious orders and ruined monasteries and abbeys. The monks were driven out of Fécamp, the abbey was set on fire and largely destroyed, and Dom Bernardo Vincelli's secret of the Benedictine Elixir seemed lost for ever.

When the storm had blown over, it was found that the monks had contrived to place in safe hands some part of the abbey treasures: gold plate, tapestries, paintings, archives and parchments which their holders carefully preserved.

Hence it was that 1863 a Fécamp merchant, Monsieur Alexandre le Grand, discovered in some manuscripts which had been bequeathed to him the parchment on which had been written the formula of the Benedictine Elixir. Working from this formula Monsieur A. Le Grand was untiring in his search for the secrets of treating and mixing plants, and after patient research and numerous tests he succeeded in reconstituting the old recipe.

Thus the precious liqueur was perfected with its exquisite taste and colour, the direct descendant of the Benedictine Elixir of Dom Bernardo Vincelli: Benedictine, the great French liqueur which together with its distinctive bottle is known throughout the world.

To give Benedictine a worthy setting, Monsieur A. Le Grand had a fine palace built in 1876 in the Renaissance style and here he gathered together many of the works of art originally housed in the old abbey.

100.000 visitors each year pass though the rooms of this museum and are also shown the distillery where Benedictine is prepared according to the old formula, but with the best of modern methods.

Bishop Saint Eloi :
polychrome wood
(XVII century).

THE MUSEUM

The Benedictine buildings form an ideal framework for a distillery and a museum. The founder, Alexandre Le Grand, was anxious to save and preserve the precious remains of the Benedictine Abbey of Fécamp which had come into his possession, and it is due to him that visitors today can admire much of the abbey rood-screen and also the portraits of the abbots of Fécamp, especially that of Pierre Rogier de Roziers who was elected Pope and held office from 1342 to 1352.

Every artistic and craft activity known to the Middle Ages and the Renaissance is reprensented in these collections which have been gradually built up: there are paintings, lavishly illuminated prayer-books, precious enamels, old wainscoting, gold plate, numerous statues, some of which still retain all the freshness of their original colouring, etc. The few specimens reproduced here will give some idea of the wealth of interest the museum offers.

"In this way art and industry come together in an astonishing harmony. Each supports the other, each giving to the other its nobility and consolidating its greatness and lasting fame." (R.E. Engel).

ON THE OPPOSITE PAGE:

Pieta:
Polychrome wood (XV c.)
Martyrdom of Saint Barbara:
miracle of the locusts,
Rhenish painting (XV c.)
Reliquary:
Limoges enamel (XIII c.)
Pieta:
Limoges enamel (XV c.)
Prayer-book:
Manuscript with miniatures
(XV c.)
Norman pitchers:
pewter (XVII c.)

"BÉNÉDICTINE
la grande liqueur
française"

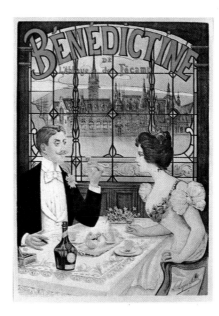

Still in current use after more than a hundred years, this slogan testifies to the reputation and continuity of a star among liqueurs.

During the last century, as advertising was still practically unknown, Alexandre Le Grand had to be both bold and confident to invest a large sum of money in publicity.

All means were employed to bring Benedictine to fame, in France as well as in foreign countries. Today, in Fecamp's publicity museum, you can retrace that effort in the exhibits of post-cards or ashtrays, pocket knives or inkstands, fans or decks of cards, and a significant collection of menus. Above all, there is a spectacular exhibit of posters bearing famous signatures: Mucha, Capiello, Lopez, Silva, Sem, and more recently, Brenet.

You can see brochures in every language, praising the qualities of Benedictine and B AND B. Be it last century posters or modern advertising, they all stress the natural spirit of Benedictine and B AND B, and their steadily increasing success.

CRÉATION : U & O PUBLICITÉ
PHOTOGRAPHY : D. EICHHORN
ILLUSTRATIONS : A. LE POLLOTEC

ACCESSORIES : BACCARAT, BOUTIQUE DANOISE, DESIGN, LA MOISSON, MAGASINS RÉUNIS,
MUSÉE DES CAVES DE LA TOUR EIFFEL, PUIFORCAT, PORTHAULT.

ACHEVÉ D'IMPRIMER
SUR LES PRESSES DE LA SOCIÉTÉ NOUVELLE IMPRIMERIE MODERNE, NANTES
EN SEPTEMBRE 1973